This book belongs to

Sherri Evans

About the Author

Born and raised in Springfield, Illinois, Katie Raynolds Johnson has a special affinity for her hometown and its hero, Abraham Lincoln. Her parents, sisters, brother, aunts, uncles, cousins, and friends are all shining examples of why Springfield means "good people." Katie now lives in the Lincoln Square neighborhood of Chicago, Illinois, with her husband, Jeff, and daughter, Paisley.

Katherine Johnson / Paisley Publishing

Chicago, Illinois

www.goodnightspringfield.com

ISBN 978-0-615-79841-7

© 2013 Katherine Raynolds Johnson

All rights reserved.

No portion of this book may be used or reproduced by any means or in any medium without the prior written permission of the publisher.

Goodnight Springfield

By Katie Raynolds Johnson

Good morning, Springfield!

What a wonderful day.

Let's see the city,

and let Abe lead the way!

Abraham Lincoln was the best president . . .

FEDERAL RESERVE NOTE
THE UNITED STATES OF AMERICA
C93195601A
FIVE
C
C93195601A
WILL PAY TO THE BEARER ON DEMAND
FIVE DOLLARS

He's on five dollar bills,
and also one cent.

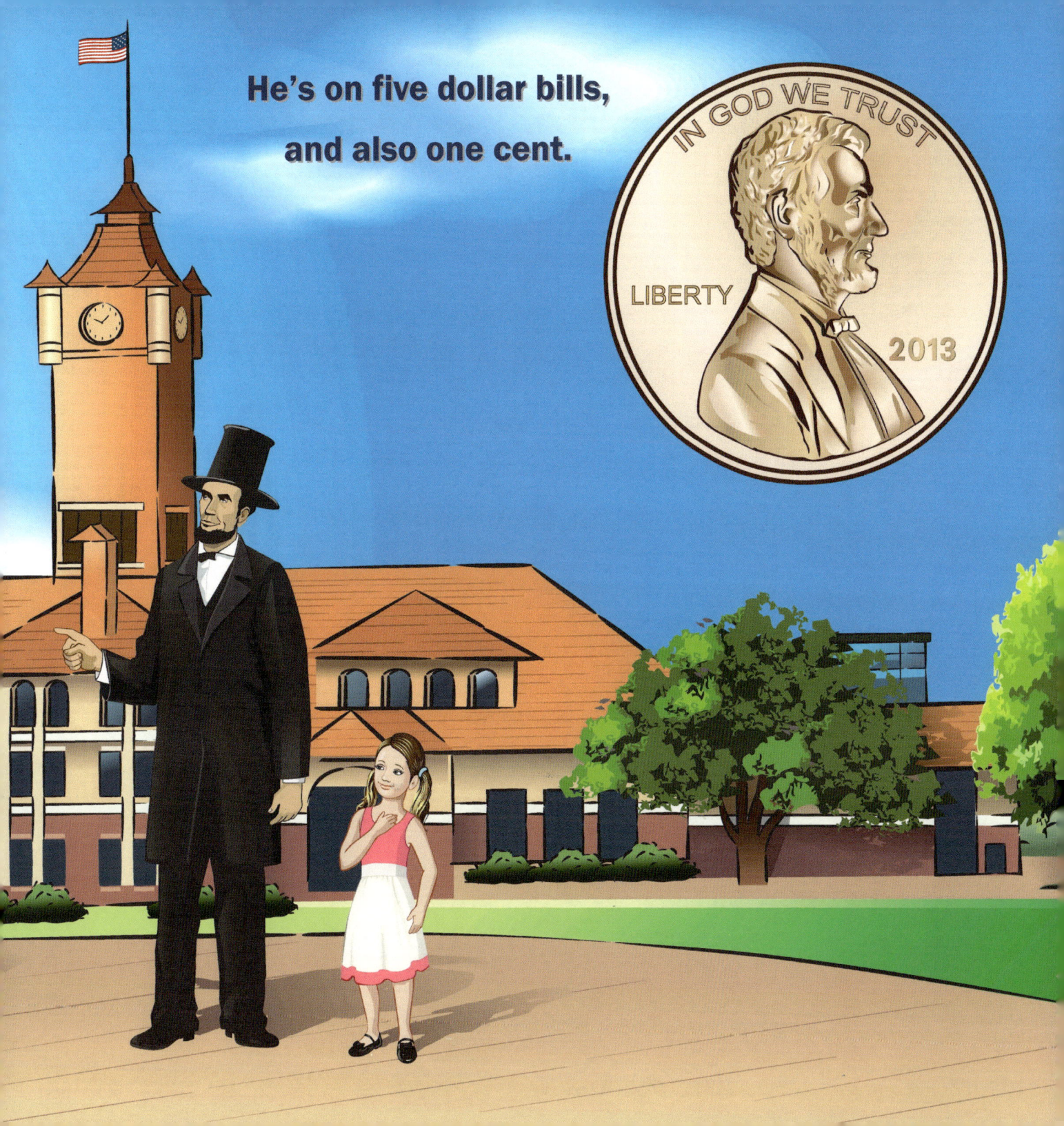

Our journey begins

with a tour of his past.

LINCOLN-HERNDON LAW OFFI

Where he lived,
and he worked,
and was buried at last.

A museum and library now honor his life.

There you can learn about his kids and his wife.

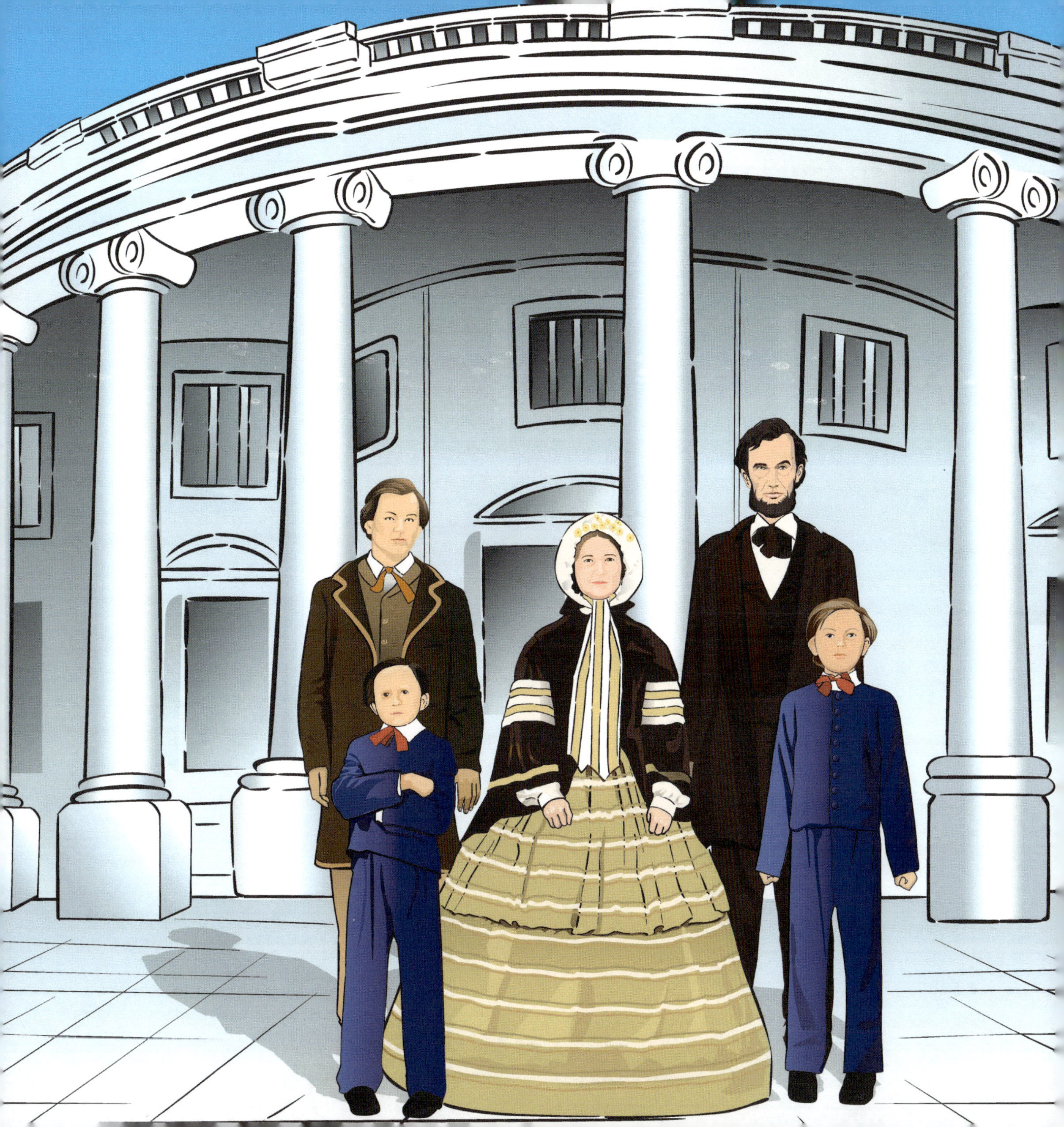

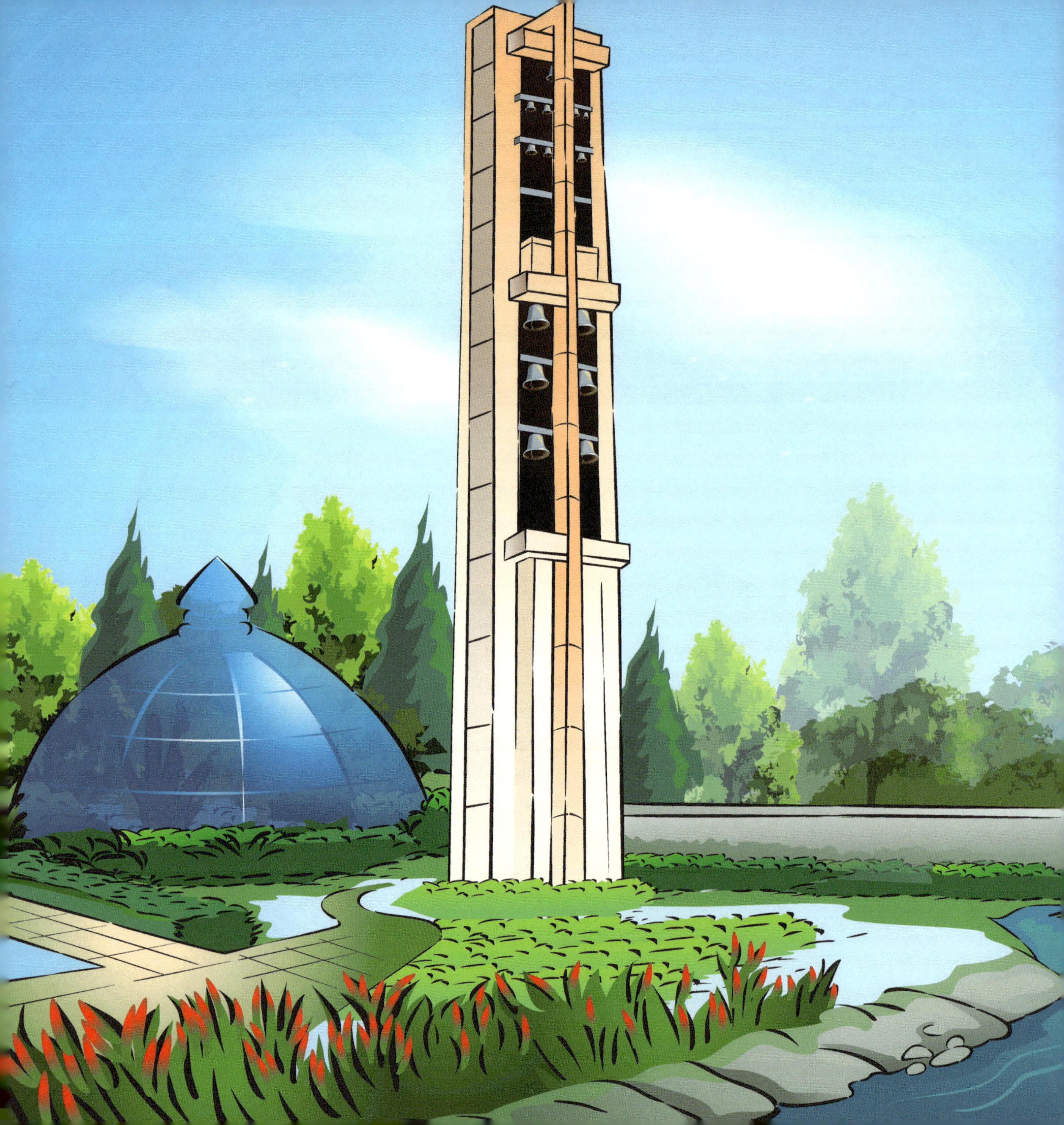

Next on our list, what will we see?

Parks full of flowers, bells, ducks, and trees.

If we want to get wet

or ride on a boat,

Lake Springfield is where

we can swim or just float.

It's time to eat lunch, so what shall we do?

Eat corn dogs or chili or a yummy horseshoe!

Springfield is the capital of the whole state.

At the Capitol Building, lawmakers debate.

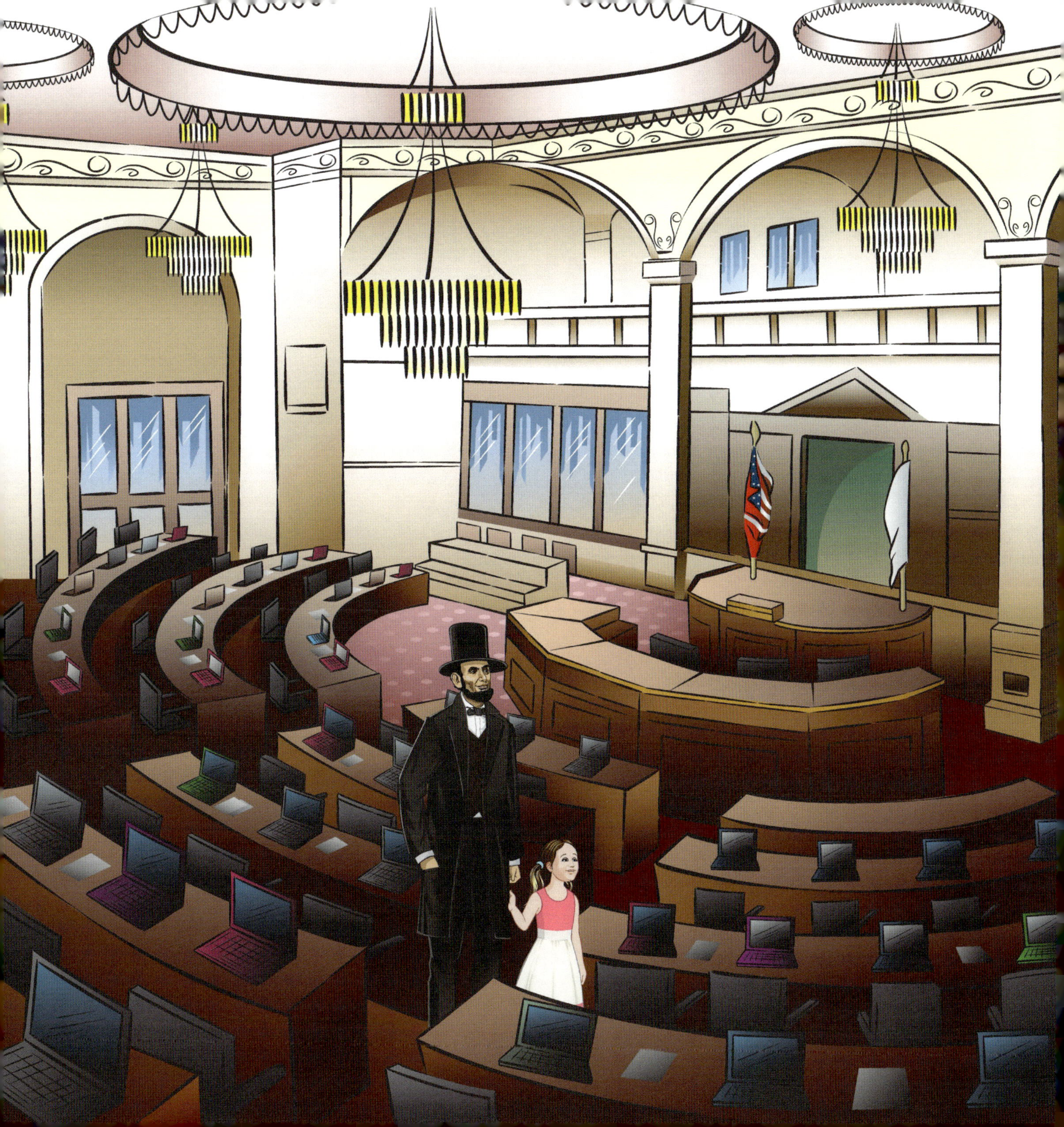

The Dana-Thomas House is a historical site.

A beautiful home designed by Frank Lloyd Wright.

Students take classes at U of I.

The Muni shows plays under the evening sky.

Each year Springfield hosts the Illinois State Fair. A butter cow, concerts, and games – it's all there!

Illinois State Fair

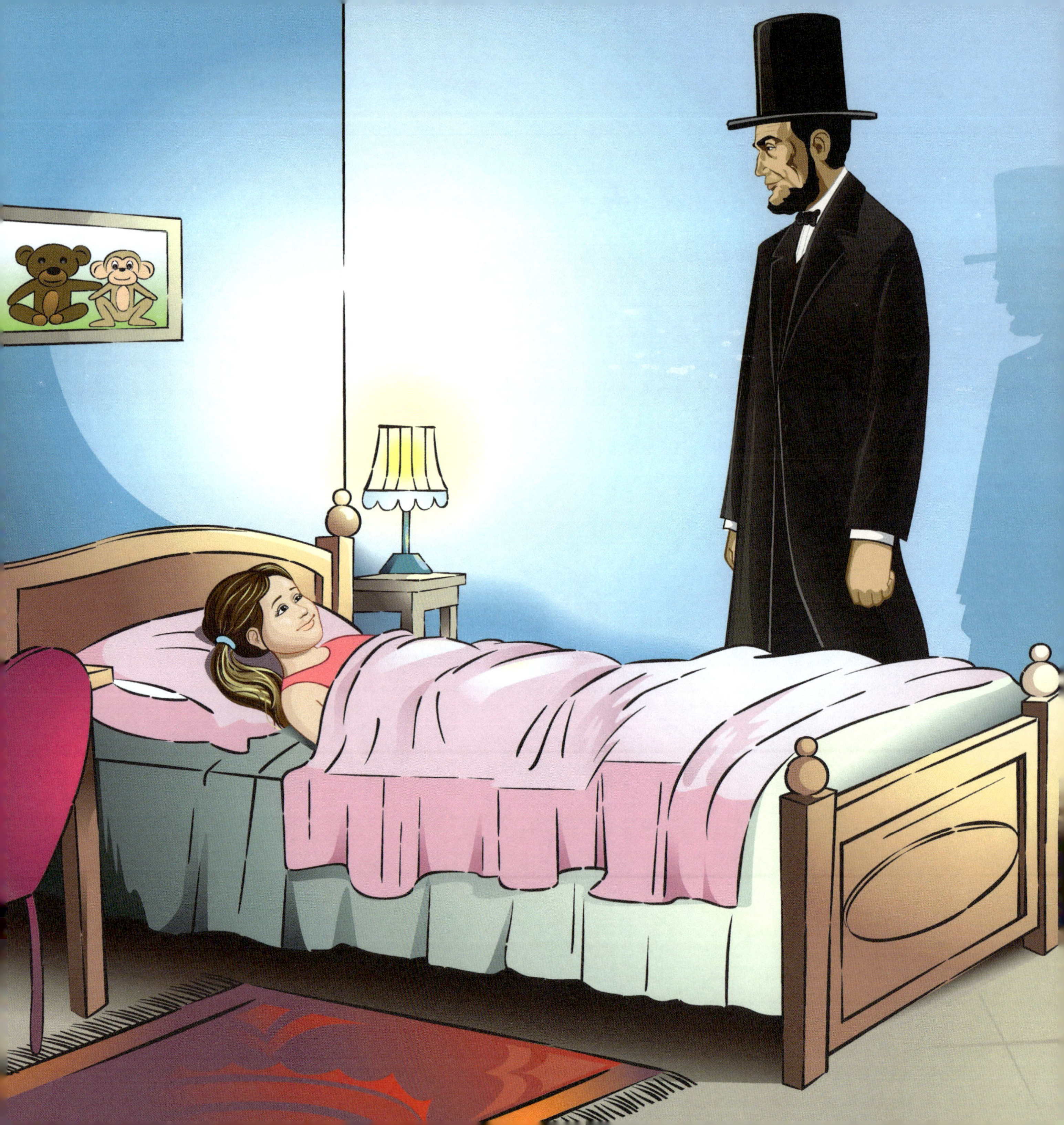

What a great day!

It has been just right.

But now it's time to say goodnight.

Tucked in my bed, I'll drift off to sleep.

Dreaming of Springfield,

and the memories I'll keep.

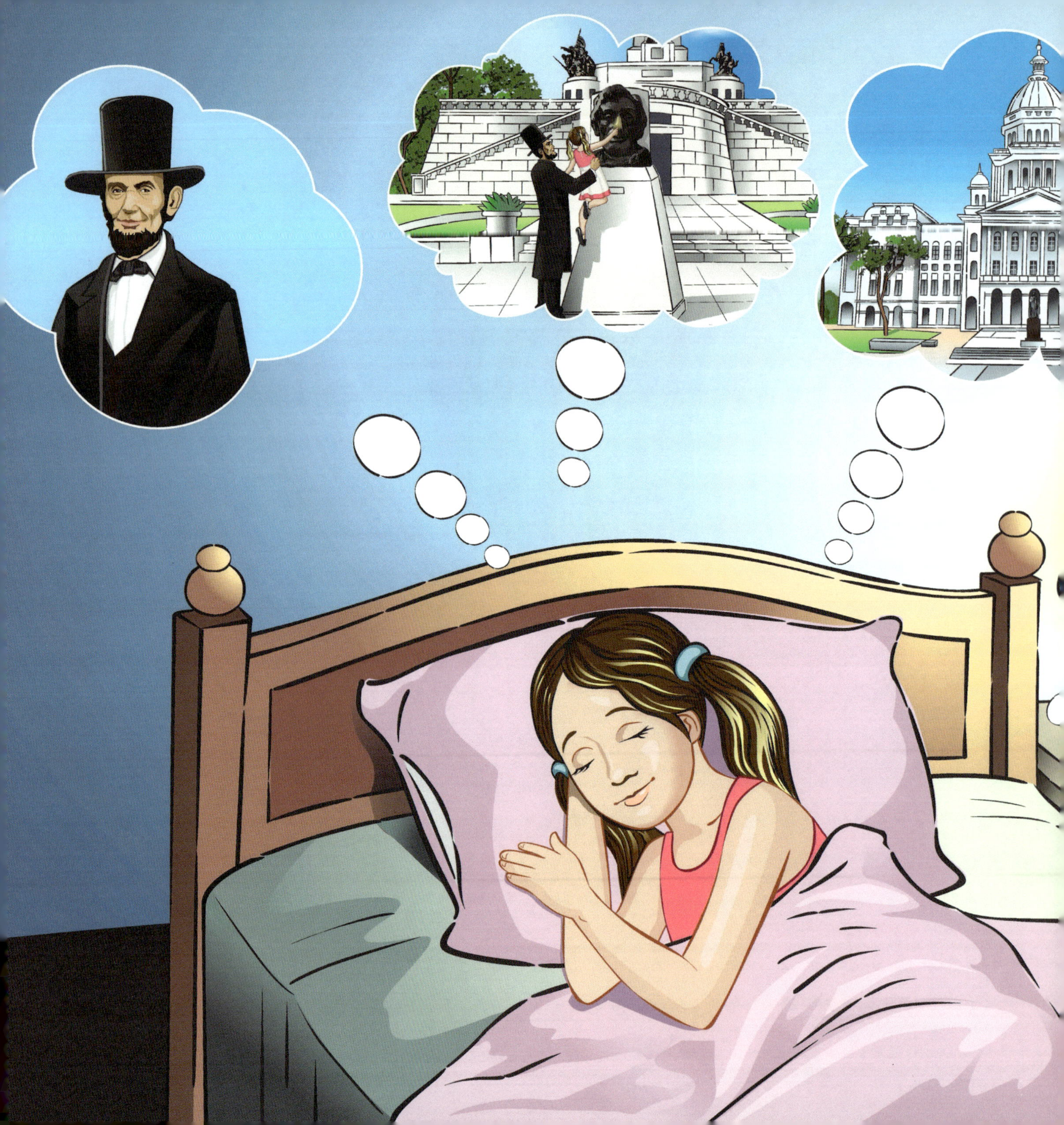

Goodnight Mr. Lincoln.
Goodnight Lincoln sites.
Goodnight Capitol Building.
And plays shown at night.

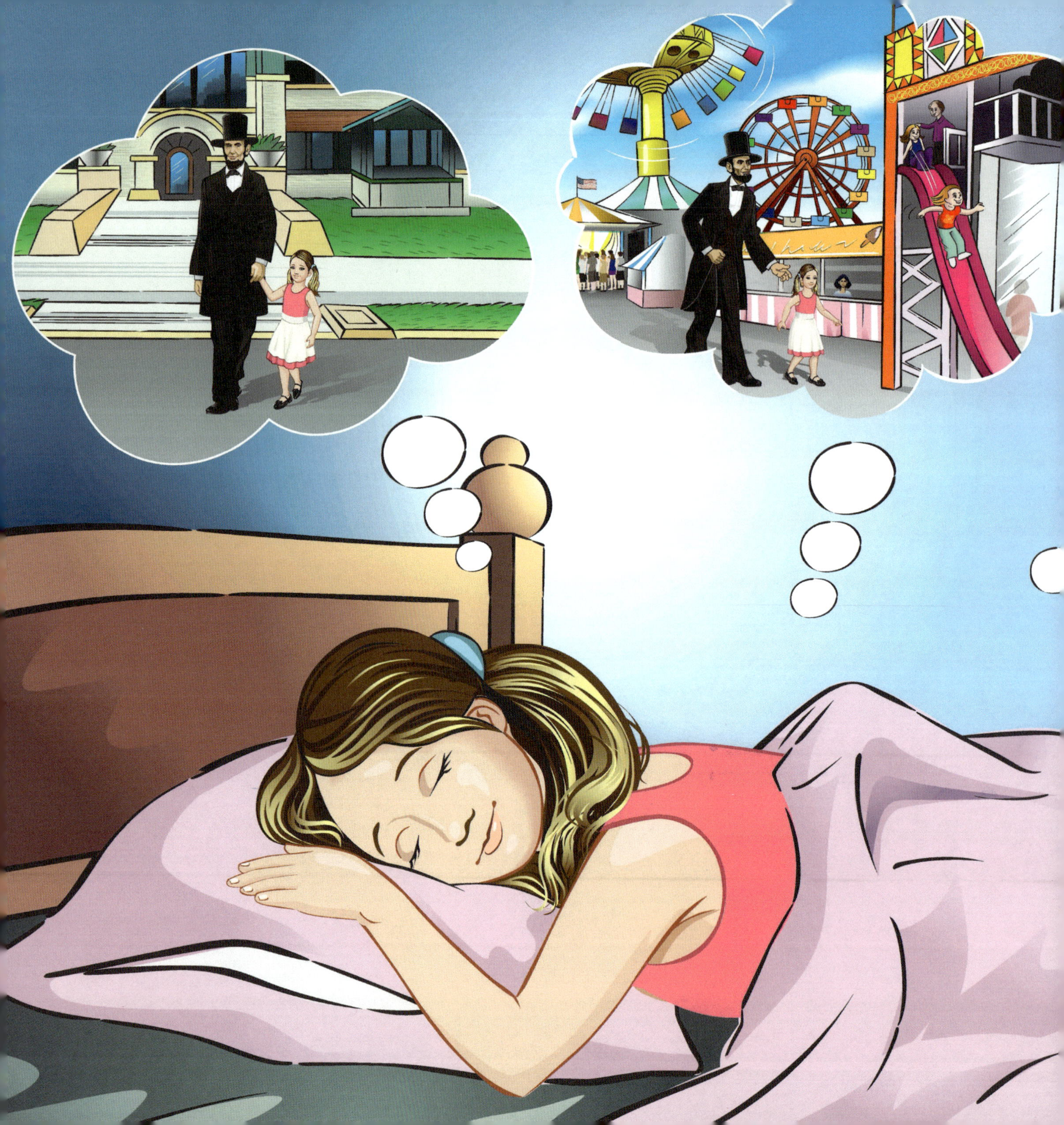

Goodnight Dana-Thomas House.

Goodnight State Fair.

Goodnight parks and boat rides.

Goodnight everywhere.

For Jeff and Paisley.

**Thank you to my loving parents,
Lynn and Randy.**

Made in the USA
Charleston, SC
15 October 2013